Poems

CHRISTOPHER LEE BOWEN

Poems

CHRISTOPHER LEE BOWEN

ARPress
ILLUMINATING IDEAS
EMPOWERING VOICES

ARPress
45 Dan Road Suite 5
Canton MA 02021

Hotline: 1(888) 821-0229
Fax: 1(508) 545-7580

Ordering Information:

Quantity sales. Special discounts are available on quantity purchases by corporations, associations, and others. For details, contact the publisher at the address above.

Printed in the United States of America.

ISBN-13:   Paperback   979-8-89330-386-5
              eBook   979-8-89330-387-2

Library of Congress Control Number: 2024902949

Contents

Foreword

'Poetry is a collaboration between readers and author. The author writes his impressions and understanding of a given subject but relies on the imagination of the reader to share and explore the implications of his words. Although we are separated by time and distance, a spiritual and emotional bond is achieved when author and reader share the epiphany of a poem.'

International Airport

This nowhere, a contrived freedom
expatriate as air,
demonstrates our mastery
of what we meet or leave behind.

Each precise beginning
finds an ending imprecise,
as we fly to where or whom we wish
only to find them somehow less.

The conquered distance
returns within ourselves
as all that's joined grows relative
becomes a nowhere too.

Until the town seems smaller
the loving eyes less absolute.

Yucatan, etc.

Cortez, DeMille are gone.
It's now the locus
of postgraduate honeymoons,
urban fugues, a minor literary genre.

Knowledge and ejection predispose us
to technological parody—
antique busses, burros, plumbing, pyramids,
as if nothing ever caught on.

There is no CHRONOLOGY, the pace and mores
are too counterproductive—
poster Indians pee along the road,
the women never dust.

We like the Sartrean-Spanish askewness—
bugs, sex, dysentery, moonlight—
as if, though settled with us,

the Fates vacation here.

My Love

Thought tells me you are no more fair
than sunlight seen through dappled leaves
your walk bears no more startling grace
than fawns at play in morning air.

The colors of your cheek no more surprise
than flowers on a wild green hill
and stars no more amaze the night
than I am by your eyes.

Your touch falls no more gently down
than butterfly upon the rose
the Celtic harp at twilight sounds
as lovely as your voice at dawn.

A lingering Summer's day in June
spreads as much warmth as does your smile
strands of your hair combine with no more grace
than branches dancing beneath the moon.

But thought compares what it can see
heart hears songs that thought can never see.

Gift

What can I give, what thing of use
that you might see or wear
would long remind so lovely you
of so loving me,
since fondness tied to use
soon fades by daily handling?
And what of words that have no use,
whose meaning all depends?
Might they find passage to your heart,
place there a sight or sound
so gentle loving fair
it now and then must rise
like music to your ear
or sunlight to your eyes
'til I am part of what you see
or part of what you hear?

Autumn Song

*Winter's edge begins to cull
our lovely, pregnant aching Autumn,
swollen with Summer's fruit and
wild wind-sown berries of Spring.
Autumn is almost more than we can bear,
all memory of beauty, grace and light,
of promise kept, or not, and ripeness in decline.
Smells of slow decay hint at April's green
and rusting leaves recall
branching glories of the Spring.*

*Sun-drunk pears startling all the wild amazed birds
leap through frosted air like rainbows,
yellow, rose and gold,
to spread their final sunburst over
chill-threatened Earth.
The pears were not taught, do not expect,
harbor from ice-bladed wind.
So gathered by your hands they glow
wondering, silent, through slanting afternoons
amazed by the warmth of your voice,
your touch, your love,
their second un-hoped for
Summer in the Sun.*

Mao I

(After an ink drawing by Mao I,
Song Dynasty circa 1100, in
Freer Gallery of Oriental Art)

Faded, brown, discrete,
as flowers pressed
in some antique book or magazine
between timeless print grown meaningless,
suggest an intimate mood—
fleeting, flown, perennial,
his femur sausage-linked bamboo
or subtle joint-less trout, lightly inked,
survived the arson and the coups d'états.
We find no window-sized Madonna
or noble with fluffed moustache
winking across the room
at a Burgher winking back.
Here on a silk pane, light-boned swallows
toss in wind-sifted willows,
while at wind-arrested edge of flight one flies
caught forever turning in his almond eyes.

Lute

Curved, inviting, light
it has the look of antique ships,
a galleon bulge of straight-grained wood.
Fretful cat-gut cords coiled taut
by silver screws above the calibrated neck
conceal a hundred foot-pound pirouette.
Child of Sirocco and Spain,
veils, fans, brocade and lace,
olive, vine, and orange surprise,
its plangent tones irrigate the moonlit air,
peek through black-eyed jalousies.
Dowland, Cutting, and solid Bach
crocheted arabesques of tuneful notes
like pearls, rubies, emerald stones
to pluck or tease from that dark pupil
a winking smile of treble Sun.

Nam

Missouri volunteers bit bullets, watched,
as Santa Ana's baggage washed
their brazen hair, hip deep
in the Rio Grande.
The ancient river moved across the land
like slow drool down a leather cheek.

Bang! Paul Bunyon's balls
rolled down the Great Divide, rattled
across the porcelain sea.
Oh the girls!
Hair hot and black. Whoopee!
Their tongues as pink as baby fat.

Now tongs drop a hissing crepe
on the defoliated plate. Butter complicates
our fingers, soils the bib.
We crack a claw. Like a crib
at Benin, wary and dull,
the eagle fills his nest with skulls.

Guadacanal 2019

Tour boat, ice-blue water.
Five rubber rafts,
12 heroes each, approach
Antarctic beach.
Explorer: 'Look! Penguins!'
Rest chirp approval, focus Canons,
shoot penguins left and right.
'Great! Wonderful!'
Two hours later, 3-star restaurant,
Tierra del Fuego.
'Global warming…'
from the end of the table.
Heads nod pious assent. Crab dinner,
Sauvignon Blanc. 'This is great!' 'Wonderful!'
Are they talking about the crab?
Or the penguins?
Does it matter?

Descent

The engram in our genes
has found
the opposing thumb and descent from trees
empirically sound,
but being pragmatic denies KULTUR
an Imprimatur.

NOTHING SUBTLE WORKS

is Nature's theme,
though guile improve Aesop's fox
and men are warned by dream,
that still saves the paradox—
success and failure are narrow views
rigorously pursued.

Woods

In the green woods no path has direction,
decay is a form of progress
and, despite all the circumspection,
'Getting there' wouldn't be understood.
It's true, ants industrialize and squirrels,
very middle class, bank on prodigal oaks.

But the basic fashion is Baroque--
tulips like Venetian glass,
pearl violets and Queen Anne's lace.
Birds ignite on every branch,
each elm has Restoration sleeves,
and the bees and flowers are an old scandal.

The effort, what there is, doesn't show.
Flying must be fun. Memories are short,
and where nothing is remembered,
nothing is routine.
Everyone has a talent. Nests seldom fail
and what's spent is miraculously retained.

What they report of us, we have only
indignant noises from which to judge--
and then the quiet watching until we go.

Then and Now

Then, I did not know that you were there
or miss the slight confusion of your hair
or think about your gracious smile
when pausing by a brook a while.

Or wandering under cloud-blown skies
did not recall the beauty of your eyes.
When walking in the woods in June
through green-filled Summers in full bloom

I did not think of how you walk
or of the music of your talk.
(So like sunlight over fields of flowers.)
Now, strolling over fields for hours

I forget what once had been.
Your beauty in my heart has so grown
you now are all the Spring times I have seen
and all the Summers I have known.

Flesh

See where it burns in Titian's brush,
subsides along cool Aegean stone,
or twists in the fist-faces of Rome,
our only mystery--flesh.

There uncertainty ends
or does it merely pause?
The surgeon's knife reveals a shadow
no surface contains. Our laws are not
what we do or vow.

Yet, surface is all, and scars--
the scuttled pains that heal.
Observe how memory collects in flaws
placed where they are most real,
or how, as flowers the persistent leaf
bears the color of its grief.

My Words

I have only words to tell
the meanings of my heart—
no glance or touch to guide me
to your own.
Other's verses, like an uncle's suit,
got second hand
and shaped to other angles
resist my heart's intent,
don't fit or sound or feel
the way I do.
All my heart intends slips
through their lines like
silver fish through sea-green nets.
But somehow my heart trusts
my words to shape
your beauty in my mind
marveling at metaphors of gold and light
that name you rose and sun
and shining star.

Your Silence

Cruel fair, where will your beauty go
when stars desert the night
and birds no longer sing,
when silence stills the trees
and green has passed us by,
unless it find a home within my heart
where I can keep your summer green
against the snow and cold
and silent dark?

Cruel fair, how will they then recall
your beauty from the night
when rainbows disappear
and peach and plum and pear
fall to grass turned brown,
unless it find a home within my words
and they in turn survive to speak you fair
against the snow and cold
and silent dark?

London Winter Fantasy

Can they not see how daffodils
spring up to greet you where you walk,
how rays of early morning light
twine red roses in your hair,
how as you pass the sky above
fills with Sun and Summer blue,
how street lamps turn to apple bowers
or palms that bend to serve you dates
and Nelson nods as you go by?

How your voice plays lutes of air
that eager song birds flock to hear,
how deer stroll New Cross Road en route
to nibble apples from your hand
while here my heart like some wild bird
fills the air with beating wings
wanting to tell them what they missed
what I have somehow heard and seen.

Freudiana

Famous poet Barclay Cruse
current toast of New York salons
wears tinted glasses and Italian shoes
and composes doggerel for subway johns.

Acclaimed a purist by his colleagues
hard-edge painter Geoffrey Pyle
earned during summers spent at Antibes
covert commissions from Armstrong tile.

Junk sculptor Cranston Bold
collects mufflers and I'm told
often edits his creations
to fix his Chevy station wagon.

Cordell composes way-out music
quartets for flute and flushing toilets.
his father was a music critic
and caned him with his clarinet.

Ethics

Taught accurately to account
for each reward an exact amount
a Kantian conscience reprehends
a stray Romantic dividend.

Publicly our just desert
is measured by our type of work,
for what surgeons are forgiven
clerks and watchmen go to prison.

Few are ushered through the streets
in black sedans by the police
to carpeted chambers where the great
decide the future of the State.

Love, Genius, Power are for the elect.
Underpaid and oversexed,
most lives are lived where intersect
the ragged lines of job and sex.

So if future preference won't assuage
your trussed Byronic middle age
think of all the lions who
are languishing in Christian zoos.

A Kind of Winter

Never to see you turn and smile
Or smell your rain-wet hair
Or feel your hand or hear your voice
Or look into your heart-full eyes
Or hold you when you cry
'til Sun and laughter come again
is a kind of Winter, as now
when city, meadow, river, field
are numb with cold and lashed by rain
that bends us in rebuke of our
too prodigal Spring.
But Sun and Spring will come again
painting trees and flowers, grass and sky
green yellow red and blue
and water freed from ice and snow
will dance seaward through clover fields
past celebrating birds to sunlit shores
where my wildly beating heart
searching horizons of blue sky someday may see
your homeward sail sparkling whitely
at furthest edge of the infinite blue-green
dancing sea.

Beach Boys

Male, wise-virgin sly
within their pubic-awkward
brawn, they testify
to ultimate, wry-caricatured
innocence of flesh.

The body? Yes. But strutting chaste
And mirror brave—enough
for mirror bluff.
None dares to risk,
or daring, could but hate

A dim-lit face-to-face
With female want-flesh Odalisque.